# ESSENTIAL SPORTS

ESSENTIAL SPORTS – FOOTBALL
was produced by

**David West** 人人 **Children's Books**
7 Princeton Court
55 Felsham Road
London SW15 1AZ

*Designer:* Rob Shone
*Editor:* James Pickering
*Picture Research:* Carlotta Cooper

*First published in Great Britain by* Heinemann
Library, Halley Court, Jordan Hill, Oxford
OX2 8EJ, part of Harcourt Education.
Heinemann is a registered trademark
of Harcourt Education Ltd.

07 06 05 04 03
10 9 8 7 6 5 4 3 2 1

ISBN 0 431 17371 0 (HB)
ISBN 0 431 17378 8 (PB)

British Library Cataloguing in Publication Data

Smith, Andy
Football. - (Essential Sports)
1. Soccer - Juvenile literature
I. Title
796.3'34

*Printed and bound in* Italy

*An explanation of difficult words can be
found in the glossary on page 31.*

# ESSENTIAL SPORTS

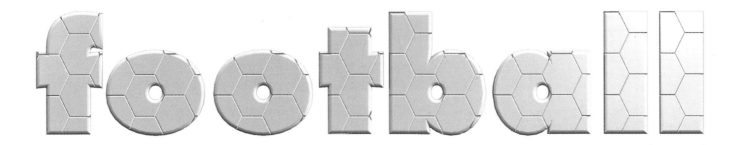

# football

## Andy Smith

Heinemann
LIBRARY

# Contents

*The Millennium Stadium in Cardiff, opened in 1999. A fine example of a modern sports stadium, it is the present home of the FA Cup Final.*

Women's football is a fast-growing international sport. Here, Sweden and Australia compete in the 1999 World Cup.

# Introduction

Football is the world's game, played in virtually every country on the planet. While the top nations and the top clubs are from Latin America and Europe, football, or soccer as it also known, is gaining strength in Africa, North America and Asia. The 2002 World Cup in Korea and Japan proved just that – Senegal, the USA and the host nations were outstanding, although, eventually, the final was between Brazil and Germany! The World Cup, played in state-of-the-art stadiums, is broadcast to massive TV audiences around the world. Teams display brilliant skills, and show just how far the sport has come since its beginnings as a rough game, often without rules. The beauty of football, though, has always been that it can be played almost anywhere by anyone – all you need is a ball.

Brazilian fans at the 2002 World Cup. They always make any match with their team a colourful occasion, and there was no doubt about their favourite player!

# History of the game

Quite how and where the game began is not known, though in China archaeologists have discovered stone balls dating from 10,000 BC, which could have been used in an early version of football.

*Calcio, an early form of the game, was played in Italy from the 15th century.*

### EARLY DAYS

Tsu-Chu-Tsu or Cuju was played in China from around 200 BC, using a stuffed animal skin for a ball, which was kicked between bamboo posts. A form of the game probably developed even earlier in South America, particularly Patagonia and Chile, while in the Amazon Basin they probably made the first rubber balls.

*Eton's school team in the 1870s. As Old Etonians, they won the FA Cup in 1879 and 1882.*

### THE FIRST CODES

Games like Knappan, played in Wales from about AD 900, and English 'mob' football, had few rules. They were played violently, the object being to move a ball from one end of a village to the other. By the 19th century, English public schools each had their own versions of the game. Common rules were not established until 1846. The Football Association, formed in 1863 to govern the game, drew up a revised version.

## THE PEOPLE'S GAME

As football became popular in public schools, it was also taken up in industrial areas. Outside London, the greatest growth was in Sheffield, home to the first 'football club' – Sheffield FC. The first FA Cup competition took place in 1871–2. In November 1872, the first international was played between Scotland and England, a 0-0 draw at Partick. The Football League was formed in 1888 – twelve clubs from the North and Midlands.

*After 1888, regular fixtures were played between the clubs in the new Football League.*

*Sir Stanley Matthews was one of only three men to play for England before and after the Second World War.*

*Uruguay won the first World Cup at home in 1930, and again in 1950.*

## THE WORLD'S GAME

British sailors and merchants took the FA rules with them to all parts of the world, and in 1904 the Federation Internationale de Football Association – 'FIFA' – was established to govern the world game. Football became an Olympic Sport at the 1908 Games in London. The first World Cup was held in 1930.

England's Football League had grown to four divisions of professional clubs by the outbreak of war in 1939.

## MODERN TIMES

Over 140 years after the world's first Football Association was established in England, the game, including women's football, is more popular than ever. Matches in the Premier League are broadcast in 164 countries. About 5 billion people watched the 2002 World Cup, fascinated by stars like Ronaldo and Zidane. The growth of super clubs like Manchester United, Real Madrid and AC Milan – made wealthy by television money, sponsorship and fanatical support – seems unstoppable. By 2000, 204 countries were affiliated to FIFA.

*Television coverage of football has improved as the game has grown in popularity.*

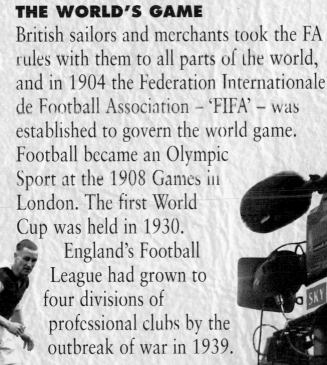

# Kit

The first professionals in the late 19th century would scarcely recognise today's game – especially the modern day kit.

### BALLS

If it is true that an early Chinese form of the game used stone balls, there was no chance that any ancient Chinese midfielder would be able to 'bend it like Beckham'. Players in the early 20th century had a hard task to kick the ball any distance in wet or muddy conditions. Made from leather panels stitched around a rubber bladder, the ball soon absorbed water and became very heavy. Heading the ball with its exposed lace was only for the brave-hearted and hard-headed!

*Ouch! Heading the old, heavy, leather ball was often a painful experience.*

*The ball should be between 68 and 70 cm in circumference and weigh 425 g.*

### TECH TIPS – STUDS, BLADES AND PIMPLES

*Modern lightweight football boots, built for speed and control, have various studs for different conditions. Rubber studs are used on hard ground, aluminium for grip on slippery ground, while blades and nylon screw-in studs are used when a pitch is firm with a soft top. On indoor and artificial pitches, boots with pimpled soles are worn.*

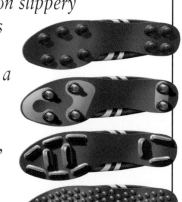

### THE MODERN BALL

Modern balls are made in various ways. Leather has largely been replaced by modern synthetic materials, producing a lighter, more aerodynamic ball. Before 1950, a football had only twelve panels, which meant that it soon went out of shape. These days, balls have twelve five-sided and 20 six-sided panels. This ensures that the ball keeps its shape and is easier to control, and with no exposed stitching, it is not painful to head.

### OLD BOOTS

In the early days of football, players wore heavy, industrial-type footwear with studs nailed into the soles. Wealthier players could afford to have boots specially made, but it was still thought that the heavyweight styles were the best, with the ankles well protected. Influenced by the boots worn by Brazilian and Hungarian players, lighter boots became available in the 1950s.

*To kick the old ball any distance required a heavyweight boot and thick shin pads for protection.*

*A modern football boot weighs no more than 250 g.*

*Strips made from modern 'breathable' textiles help to keep players cool.*

*Shin pads have become lighter.*

*Some players wear cycling shorts underneath their strip to protect their thigh muscles.*

*Football shirts are not just for the players! The fans wear them with their favourite's name and number emblazoned on the back.*

### NEW BOOTS

Old boots were made of leather, but modern versions are three times lighter, thanks to the use of synthetic material and the removal of the ankle protection to give the foot more flexibility.

### STRIPS

A hundred years ago, players wore long pants, thick stockings with outside shin pads and caps. The caps were sometimes the only way of identifying a player on the same side! By the 1950s, baggy shorts were common, socks were woollen and shirts were of heavy cotton. In the 1960s, shorts became shorter, socks were synthetic and shirts were close fitting. Today, sponsorship means that there is more lettering on players' shirts than ever.

2003

1970s

1940s

1860s

9

# Rules of the game

In its early days, football had very few rules, or laws. As the game became more sophisticated, rules were introduced for the sake of consistency and order.

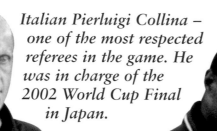

*Italian Pierluigi Collina – one of the most respected referees in the game. He was in charge of the 2002 World Cup Final in Japan.*

## RULES AND THE REFEREE

The referee is in charge, his decision being final. With the help of two assistant referees, he enforces the laws, penalising the offending team, cautioning (yellow carding) offending players where necessary or sending off (red carding) players for the more serious offences.

## THE ASSISTANT REFEREES

Assistant referees indicate by using flags when the ball is out of play and which side is entitled to the corner-kick, goal-kick or throw-in. They also advise the referee on offside decisons (see page 16), and when and where fouls are committed. A fourth official on the touchline oversees substitutions and is in charge of the 'technical areas' around the teams' benches.

*Assistant referees used to be known as 'linesmen'.*

# FOULS AND INJURIES

A foul is when a player kicks, trips, jumps at, holds, pushes or hits an opponent. Handling the ball is also a foul, resulting in a direct free kick, or a penalty if the offence is inside the penalty area. The referee decides whether or not to stop play if a player is injured, adding time to the standard 45 minutes of each half if necessary ('injury time').

*Foul! Tackling the player rather than the ball.*

*The referee's essentials. Some play safe by carrying spares of everything required.*

## THE REF'S EQUIPMENT

The days when a referee would take to the pitch armed with only a coin, a whistle and a watch have gone. Red and yellow cards, a notebook and pencil are now also necessities and a spare watch is advisable. The ref's kit must be completely different from that worn by both sides (including the goalkeepers).

SPORT

### TECH TIPS – OUT OF PLAY

*Unlike some other sports, the ball in football is only out of play when it is completely over the line. This also applies when a goal is scored. The ball is out if it goes over the line, whether it touches the ground or not.*

*In play*

*Out of play*  *Ball is now out of play*

# Pitch and positions

Running all over the pitch will just get you tired (and probably lose
you the game). Knowing where to play will save
energy and help you work as a team.

*Pitches used for internationals
have to follow these
measurements.*

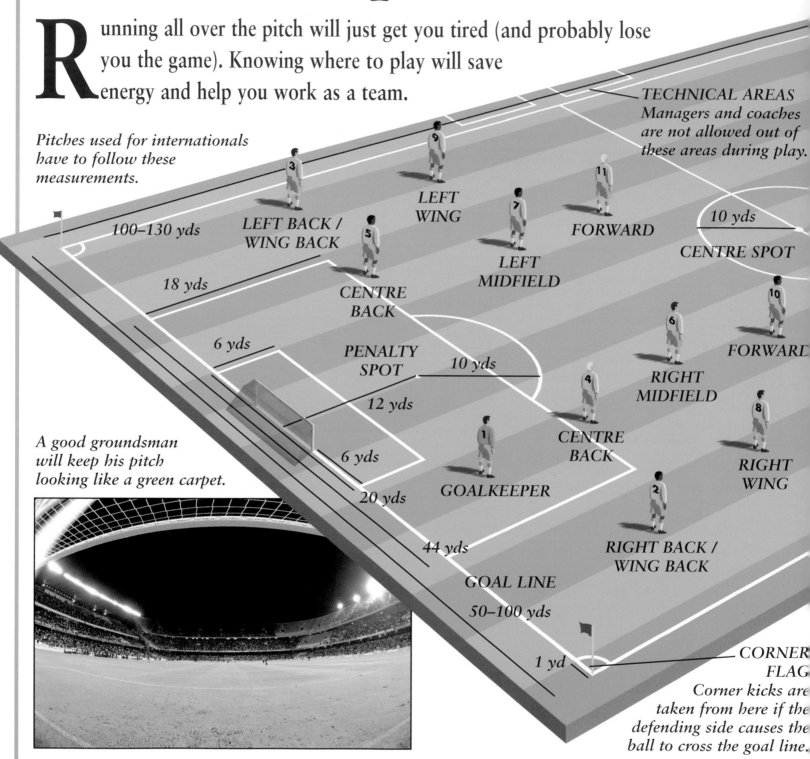

100–130 yds

18 yds

6 yds

PENALTY
SPOT

12 yds

6 yds

20 yds

44 yds

GOAL LINE

50–100 yds

1 yd

10 yds

LEFT BACK /
WING BACK

LEFT
WING

FORWARD

CENTRE SPOT

CENTRE
BACK

LEFT
MIDFIELD

10 yds

RIGHT
MIDFIELD

FORWARD

CENTRE
BACK

RIGHT
WING

GOALKEEPER

RIGHT BACK /
WING BACK

TECHNICAL AREAS
*Managers and coaches
are not allowed out of
these areas during play.*

CORNER
FLAG
*Corner kicks are
taken from here if the
defending side causes the
ball to cross the goal line.*

*A good groundsman
will keep his pitch
looking like a green carpet.*

## PERFECT PITCH

It's the groundsman's job to look after the pitch.
As soon as a game is over he will mend loose
divots and check the turf for any other damage.
Parts may have to be re-seeded or even replaced.

Later on he will roll the pitch and cut the grass.
Just before a game the white lines are painted and
the pitch may be watered, as players like the ball
to 'zip' off a slightly wet and 'greasy' surface.

All the white lines are
5 inches wide.

Goalposts are set 8 yards
apart and the crossbar is
8 feet above the ground.
Posts and bar cannot be
more than 5 inches thick.

6 YARD BOX
Goal-kicks are taken
from inside this box.

THE 'D'

PENALTY AREA
Keepers cannot handle the ball outside this area
nor can they handle a ball deliberately kicked to
them by their own team mates. A penalty can be
awarded if a defending player commits a foul here.

THE TOUCHLINE
Throw-ins are taken from this line when the
ball crosses it. The side touching the ball last
gives away possession.

HALFWAY LINE

Electric
cables

Drainage
pipes

*Pitch
measurements
were drawn up in England
when imperial units (inches, feet and
yards) were used instead of metric units.
One yard equals 0.914 metres.*

*Water-logged pitches can be a
problem for both sides.*

## WHEN THE WEATHER WINS

Football can be played at any time
and in all weathers – well almost all. Too
much rain makes a pitch too wet to play on.
Frost can make it hard and dangerous, and a referee
can't do his job in thick fog. Pitches are checked before
a match to see if they are fit and safe.

## PITCH PROTECTION

Modern grounds are very different from the first pitches,
which were little more than muddy fields. Drainage
systems help to get rid of rainwater and buried electric
cables heat the soil to keep it from freezing. Even the grass is
specially chosen to suit each individual ground. A good pitch
can make it much easier for players to use all their skills.

## TECH TIPS –
## THIRDS

The pitch is often
divided into zones called
thirds. Each group of
players will know their job
in their area and how to
play with each other. They
can move into other areas
when needed.

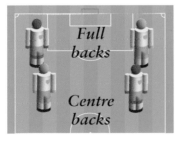
*Full
backs*
*Centre
backs*

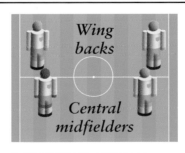
*Wing
backs*
*Central
midfielders*

*Wingers*
*Forwards*

DEFENSIVE THIRD
Centre backs are aided
by full backs on the
wing, or a 'sweeper'
can be used instead.

MIDFIELD THIRD
Central midfielders and
wing backs will try to
bring the ball forward
out of defence.

ATTACKING THIRD
Wingers can be used
instead of wing backs
to cross the ball to the
forwards in the middle.

# Goalkeeping

**G**oalkeepers are the last line of defence – just as important to the team as the star striker.

### SHOT STOPPING

The goalkeeper's most important job is to stop shots going into his goal by using any part of the body – including the hands and arms. As this frequently involves diving full length or leaping high across goal, the keeper is often the most agile player on his side. The best keepers are not only good shot stoppers, but also keep hold of the ball, not allowing chances from rebounds.

*Shout! Goalkeepers are in the best position to organise their defence.*

### TECH TIPS – KNOW YOUR ANGLES

*The goalkeeper does not have to be an expert in geometry – but sometimes it seems like that! A keeper must always be aware of where the posts are behind him, and judge the gaps that the opposition attack could shoot through to be on target. Then it's the keeper's job to use those shot-stopping skills.*

*Keepers are often better diving one way rather than the other. Practice ensures that they're capable of going in either direction.*

*The defence has left a gap through which the forward can shoot on goal.*

*Catch and hold is the best option ...*

## HANDLING

The advantage that a goalkeeper has over any other player on the field is that the hands can be used. This gives a height advantage when faced with a high cross or corner into the penalty area, and enables the keeper to defend a larger area of his goal when dealing with an opponent on the attack. The safest option for a keeper is usually to catch and hold the ball if at all possible. Otherwise, punching the ball out of the danger area, palming it wide of the net or just touching it past the post with a fingertip may be necessary.

*... when it's not, a good punch might be the answer.*

## SKILL DRILL - REFLEX SAVES

*Like every other player on the field, the goalkeeper benefits from practice. As so much of the keeper's game requires good reflexes, there are several drills which can be used to sharpen a goalkeeper's performance.*

*The keeper faces away from the opposition attack, not knowing who has the ball.*

*On a signal, he turns as the attacker with the ball shoots.*

## DISTRIBUTION

When it comes to passing the ball to a team mate, the goalkeeper is as important as any midfielder. The old-fashioned method of a keeper gathering the ball and simply booting it as far away as possible is now rarely used. To keep possession, throwing or rolling out to an unmarked team mate is seen as a better option.

# Defence

The best defenders are not just negative players. They should know what to do with the ball when they're in possession.

### WINNING THE BALL

Winning the ball fairly is a difficult skill to learn. On the ground, the defender should stay upright, eyes on the ball and judge when to take possession. In the air, it is a question of position and timing.

### TACKLING

The defenders make a clean tackle by staying with their opponent, eyes on the ball, positioning themselves to keep the attacker away from goal. When the chance comes to force the ball away from the feet of their opponent, they take it quickly. Remember – contact must be made with the ball first and attempts to tackle from behind are always penalised!

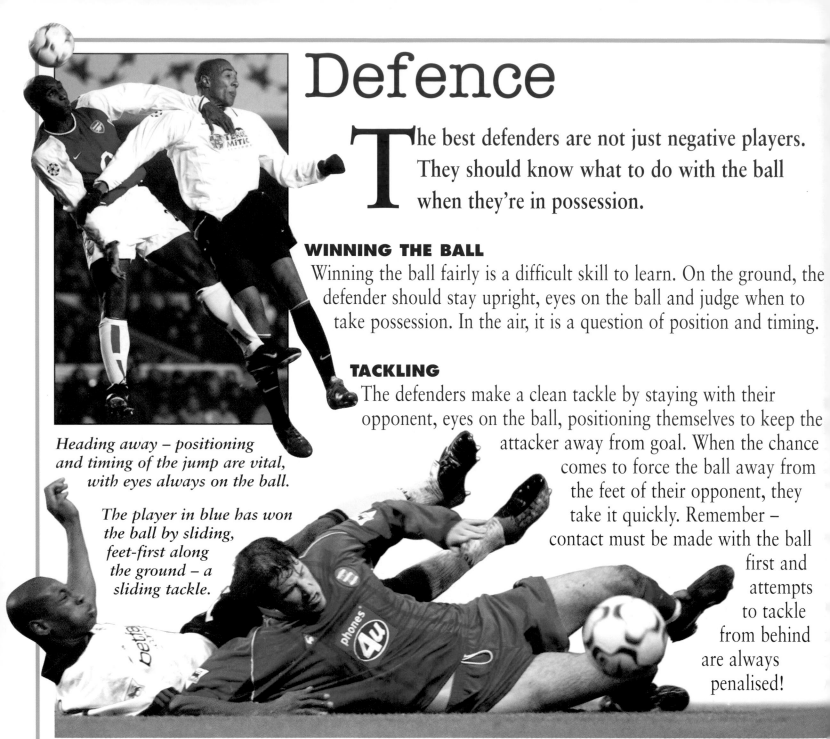

*Heading away – positioning and timing of the jump are vital, with eyes always on the ball.*

*The player in blue has won the ball by sliding, feet-first along the ground – a sliding tackle.*

---

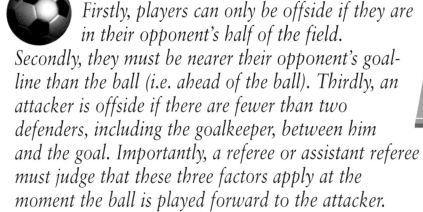

### TECH TIPS – OFFSIDE

*Firstly, players can only be offside if they are in their opponent's half of the field. Secondly, they must be nearer their opponent's goal-line than the ball (i.e. ahead of the ball). Thirdly, an attacker is offside if there are fewer than two defenders, including the goalkeeper, between him and the goal. Importantly, a referee or assistant referee must judge that these three factors apply at the moment the ball is played forward to the attacker.*

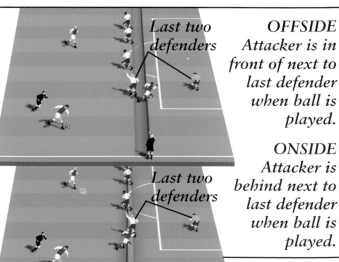

Last two defenders

Last two defenders

OFFSIDE
Attacker is in front of next to last defender when ball is played.

ONSIDE
Attacker is behind next to last defender when ball is played.

## TEAM DEFENCE

The defence is a team within the team. There is no such thing as a one-man defence. Each player at the back must be aware of the position of the others. One, usually the central defender, will be responsible for setting the line, beyond which the attackers will be caught offside. The backs (or wing backs) deal with the threat which comes down the wings, but can also turn defence into attack, receiving the throws out from the goalkeeper. The defensive wall, to protect the goal from the opposition's free kicks, is positioned by the goalkeeper, but it is the individual responsibility of the defenders in the wall to make sure none of the 'bricks' give way.

*The whole point of having a defensive wall is so that the ball has to go round, or over – never through.*

## BEING STRONG

'Being strong' doesn't mean persistent fouling – but being able to withstand the attacks of opponents without resorting to unfair methods. The basic job of a defender is to prevent the opposition having a shot at goal. The best way of doing this is to be between the attacker and the goal and, whenever possible, between the attacker and the ball.

*Make it difficult for your opponent by keeping between him and the ball.*

## SKILL DRILL – ONE-ON-ONE

*Practise with a friend, one as the attacker, the other a defender.*
*The art of timing a tackle, cleanly removing the ball from the other's possession, can best be learnt by repetition.*

*Defender waits for attacker to give chance of getting ball.*

*Attacker forced to one side, narrowing shooting angle.*

# Midfield

**M**idfielders provide the link between defence and attack, the engine room of the team.

### THE MIDFIELD GENERAL

Midfielders are usually the best all-round players on the team, capable of defending strongly and putting in tackles to win the ball. They can run, or dribble, with the ball at speed and pass accurately over long or short distances. And scoring the odd goal is useful too!

*David Beckham is the ultimate free kick specialist.*

### DEFENSIVE MIDFIELD

The first job of any midfield player is to dominate the opposition's midfielders. 'Closing down' an opponent – staying close to him and forcing him to play the ball earlier than he wants to – is one skill. Tackling to break up an opposition attack is another, but using the ball well after gaining possession is vital. The good midfielder is always aware of team mates who are in a position to receive a pass.

*Liverpool's Steven Gerrard has developed a fine all-round game.*

### TECH TIPS – STRIKING THE BALL

*To ensure maximum power and control, always use the instep, otherwise the ball could go anywhere.*

*1 Keep eyes on the ball, stay balanced.*

*2 Never lean backwards – the ball will just go up.*

*3 Make solid contact with the centre of the ball.*

*The midfield is frequently the most crowded area on the pitch. Good midfielders still find space though.*

## ATTACKING MIDFIELD

Midfielders move the ball out of their own half and into attacking positions by dribbling or passing. Keeping hold of the ball too long gives the opposition defence a chance to cover the attacking options. One long pass could catch the defence out and give the forwards a chance of a shot at goal. Or a series of short passes, drawing the defence out of position, could be effective.

## SKILL DRILL – THE ONE-TWO

*Two players working together should always beat one defender. With two short passes, the defender can be bypassed and space created for one of the attacking players to use effectively. Quick, accurate passes over a short distance work best.*

*1 Pass the ball before the defender can tackle, then move into the space.*

*2 The defender cannot cover both players, and a simple first time pass has set up an attack.*

## DECISIONS, DECISIONS

Midfielders should be capable of seeing how a move can be developed before it happens – 'vision'. In possession, a midfielder may have several options – to run with the ball before passing or shooting; to use the long ball over the defence for his forwards to run on to; or combine with team mates to draw the defence out of position and create a chance on goal. Knowing when to tackle and when to 'shadow' the opposition can stop a goal chance coming their way.

*Midfielder Jennifer Lalor of the New York Power dribbles the ball against the Atlanta Beat in 2002.*

# Attack

Scoring goals is the whole point of football, but there's more to the forward's game than just putting the ball in the net.

*Good strikers are quick to seize any opportunity to shoot at goal in a crowded area.*

*The body swerve. The ability to go either way with the ball often confuses defenders.*

## HUNTING IN PACKS

The days of a striker simply hanging around the goal waiting for the chance to score have long gone. Now strikers are even expected to help out in defence, but the main job is still creating and taking chances. To unlock tough defences, two strikers with midfield support is a most effective combination. The strikers may have different strengths, one being good in the air, the other better on the ground. Some coaches prefer two quick players working in combination to outwit the defenders.

## BEATING PLAYERS

Defenders should never allow forwards any space around the penalty box, so it's up to the attacker to find some! When it's impossible to pass to a team mate, it's necessary to take on and beat the defender. The body swerve to elude a tackle and deceive an opponent is a useful skill. With the weight on the front foot, take the ball one side of the defender, then drag it to the other side into space.

## SKILL DRILL – TAG DRIBBLING

*Learn to dribble with both feet to make your game less predictable to an opponent. With a friend in a confined area of the pitch dribble a ball each from one side to the other. Then it's a game of tag. One is 'it', the other, still dribbling a ball, has to 'tag' and take over.*

## GETTING TO THE BY-LINE

One of the best ways of creating chances for forwards is by making progress down the wings around the outside of the defence, reaching the goal line (or by-line) and pulling the ball back into the goal mouth. The defenders have to keep their backs to goal while marking the attackers and checking sideways to watch the cross coming in.

*As in all aspects of the game, attackers can't play without the ball – keep your eye on it!*

*Speedy, skilful forwards create chances.*

### TECH TIPS – CROSSES

*A good player should be able to vary the type of cross into the penalty area, depending on the position of the strikers and the defence. Against a defence strong in the air, a low, fast ball into the middle could prove effective. A hopeful lob into a crowded box rarely works.*

*1 A high cross into this area should be claimed by the goalkeeper.*
*2 A cross to a team mate in this area could entice the keeper out of position.*
*3 The short cross to a team mate able to flick a header across the face of the goal.*
*4 Long to the back post, where it can be played into areas 1, 2 or 3, or into the net!*
*5 An unmarked team mate here could have a longer range shot.*

21

# Teamwork

No player – even a genius like Pelé, Maradona or Best – could win a match on his own. Teamwork is all important.

*Teamwork starts on the training ground.*

## PLAYING FOR EACH OTHER

'All for one and one for all' – often heard, not often practised. But selfish players who play only for themselves are doing nobody any favours – except the opposition. Team spirit is an essential element of any successful team from the Champions League to the Sunday Morning League.

*Play for each other. Good team spirit can make an ordinary side good.*

⚽ **TECH TIPS – FORMATIONS**
*A good line-up can help a side play well. Which one you use may depend on your strengths, the opposition's, or even weather conditions. Teams with experience will often alter a line-up mid-game.*

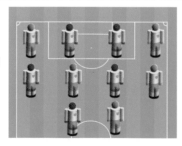

**4-4-2**
*The most common formation used, it is well balanced between attack and defence.*

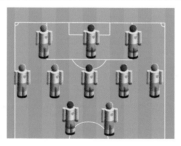

**3-5-2**
*An attacking line-up that works best with an experienced team of good communicators.*

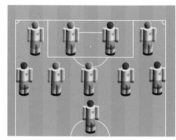

**4-5-1**
*A team protecting its lead might change to this defensive system near the end of a game.*

*Practise all the skills. Even though you may not take throw-ins regularly, a quickly taken throw might give you an advantage.*

*Whether watching in the stadium or on TV at home, you should observe the formations and patterns of play. You may learn something new.*

### SET PIECES

Both attackers and defenders should practise set pieces – a general name for corners or free kicks. The goalkeeper should organise his defence when facing a free kick. At a corner, each defender takes responsibility for marking an opposition player. A simple practice game of attack versus defence is useful for all players.

### BEING ORGANISED

Organisation on the field is one thing – being organised off it is another. Make sure your kit is in good order before you leave home, boots clean and laced. Time lost searching for missing socks or shorts would be better spent at the ground, warming up or 'kicking in'. Be ready to lend a hand with nets, flags or balls, whatever may be required to make preparation for a match that much smoother.

### SKILL DRILL – MAKING SPACE

*A player in space has more time and room to create an opening.*

*A simply-practised move in training could pay dividends in a match.*

'A' shapes to throw ball to 'B'.

'C' and 'D' make runs along touchline.

'B' turns, followed by marker.

'A' throws ball to 'C' who runs into space behind defenders.

# Going for goal

**S**coring a goal is the thing every footballer wants to do. Whether they are amazingly skilful or absurdly lucky, all goals are good.

### THE POACHER'S CRAFT

Quick thinking, fast reactions, speed, power and deadly finishing are the skills that make a goal poacher the most dangerous player in any forward line-up. The poacher uses these skills in many ways. Getting ahead of his marker in the box to meet a cross from the goal line. Receiving an accurate pass from midfield with a well-timed run into the penalty area. Being alive to any loose ball or rebound in the six-yard box and getting there first. Finishing quickly and accurately under intense pressure from defenders. Poachers are instinctive and will score in any way they can.

*Timing your jump to head the ball is essential in front of goal. Here, John Hartson wins the ball for Wales against Italy in a European Championship qualifying match.*

### SKILL DRILL – THE HALF-VOLLEY

*The half-volley (striking the ball just after it has bounced) is one of the most powerful shots there is and can often take goalkeepers by surprise. This drill will help you to time your shot to get the most power and to control it for accuracy.*

*Stand 15 m from a practice partner and take it in turns to half-volley a ball to each other. Try not to hit the ball too hard at first, concentrate on being as accurate as possible. As you become better, gradually stand further apart.*

*1 Drop a ball at your feet, keeping your eyes on it all the time.*
*2 Place your standing foot next to the ball and keep your head forward.*
*3 Using your arms for balance, strike the ball as it bounces.*
*4 Follow through with your shooting foot and practise using both feet.*

## THE SHARPSHOOTER

It takes great skill to strike a ball 23 metres and into the top corner of the goal. A keeper slightly out of position or a small gap in the defence could be all the chance you get. Stay balanced and relaxed while positioning yourself. Concentrate on direction over raw power and have the confidence to shoot. Your confidence will grow through constant practice.

*England's Alan Smith gets away from his marker.*

*Steven Gerrard scoring for England against Macedonia.*

## ALL IN THE FINISH

You may only have the goalkeeper to beat, or a cross has given you a chance in the area, but the job is not over until you have scored. Decide quickly how you are going to finish. Stay calm and always hit the target. A parried ball may bounce back to you. And be aware of who's around you – a team mate might be better placed to score.

*When successful, the bicycle kick can be very spectacular.*

### TECH TIPS – CURLING SHOTS

*Clear, long-range shots are rare during a match. More often than not, there will be defenders in the way. Bending the ball around both defenders and keeper, and into the goal, is one answer.*

*Strike the ball slightly to one side with the instep.*

*Wrap the foot around the ball to make it spin. Here the ball will bend to the left.*

25

# Football variations

As we said at the start – football can be played virtually anywhere, anytime – all you need is a ball!

## WHERE DO OLD FOOTBALLERS GO?

Footballers who retire from the game at the top level rarely give up the sport completely. Several opt to play in local leagues, many retain an interest by playing in charity matches, some hang up their boots to go barefoot on the beach.

*Eric Cantona – from Old Trafford to Copacabana*

## BEACH SOCCER

A relatively recent addition to the televised TV soccer programmes, beach soccer is played on stretches of sand all over the world. However, it took the South Americans, and in particular the Brazilians on Copacabana Beach in Rio de Janiero, to organise proper tournaments featuring former internationals.

*In different arenas, five-a-side has different rules.*

*There is no offside rule.*

*A goalkeeper may not handle the ball outside the semicircle.*

*The goals are 5 m (16 ft) wide by 1.25 m (4 ft) high.*

*Five-a-side beach soccer – good crowds to watch good players.*

*n Britain, there are six league tournaments for artially sighted teams, held at different venues round the country between November and April.*

## BLIND FOOTBALL

Players who have impaired sight can still enjoy a game. Modifications to the rules allowing for larger balls, or balls which make a sound when rolled, enable blind people to play a form of the game that is often just as competitive as any in the Football League!

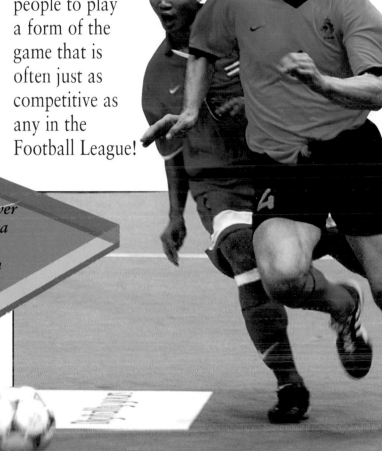

*Local rules dictate whether keepers are allowed out of the area or outfield players are allowed in.*

*There are fewer markings on a five-a-side pitch than on a full-size pitch.*

*If the ball goes out of play, it is kicked on, rather than thrown in.*

*A fast, skilful game, five-a-side helps players gain fitness.*

## TECH TIPS – ASTROTURF

*Artificial grass was developed in the USA, where natural grass could not grow in the indoor stadiums used for American football and soccer. Astroturf was installed at some league grounds in England in the 1980s, notably Queens Park Rangers, Preston and Luton, but it is now banned. It can still be seen at heavily-used parks and practice pitches.*

Rubber granules ___

Plastic 'grass'

Fibreglass weave ___

Nylon backing layer ___

Reinforced layer ___

Drainage layer ___

Base ___

## FIVE-A-SIDE

Five-a-side football was introduced to give players an indoor game in bad weather. Everton used five-a-side as a regular part of training in the 1930s, when they discovered it made them fitter and faster. Recently, tournaments have been staged featuring league teams and retired professionals.

# The world of football

The pinnacle of the world game is the FIFA World Cup, but there are many more championships for clubs and countries where players can earn their moment of glory.

### WORLD CUP

Staged every four years since 1930, except during the Second World War, Brazil have won the competition five times, Italy and West Germany three times each. The initial World Cup attracted only 13 entrants and no British team took part. By contrast, for the 2002 World Cup, over 200 countries were in the qualifying stages. South American countries have been competing for the Copa America since 1916, while the African Nations Cup was established in 1957. The European Championship started in 1960.

### INTERNATIONAL VENUES

England's most famous international venue – Wembley Stadium – has been derelict since 2000, but there are plans to build a new arena to stage all England's home internationals and the FA Cup Final. Countries prefer to use their best club grounds for internationals. In Italy they have a wide choice including Milan's San Siro and the Stadio Delle Alpi in Turin. Spain use Real Madrid's Bernabeau and Barcelona's Camp Nou amongst others.

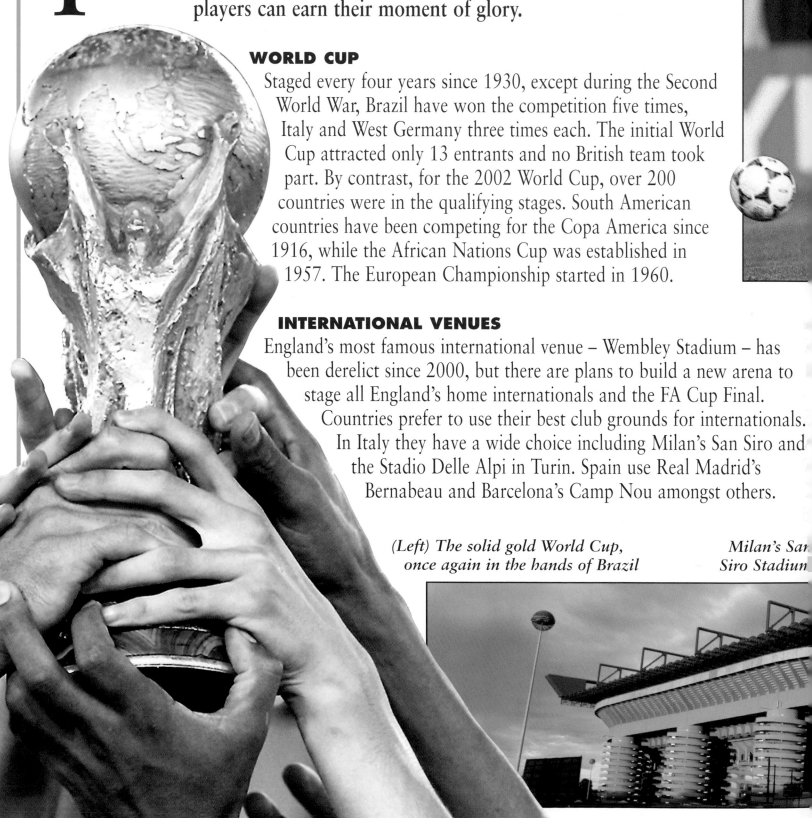

*(Left) The solid gold World Cup, once again in the hands of Brazil*

*Milan's San Siro Stadium*

*China and Norway, along with the USA, have dominated women's international football since 1991.*

## CLUB AND COUNTRY

The UEFA Champions League is regarded as the toughest club competition in the world. Depending on past performances, up to four clubs from any European country can compete for the trophy. Spain's Real Madrid have won the European Cup a record nine times. England's most successful club is Liverpool, who are four-times winners.

*Celtic, here in yellow shirts, made progress from the third round of the UEFA Cup when they beat Celta Vigo of Spain in December 2002.*

## WOMEN'S INTERNATIONAL FOOTBALL

Women's football has been played since the late 19th century, but it was not until 1957 that the International Ladies' Football Association was formed and the Manchester Corinthians won the Women's European Championship. The first Women's World Cup was held in China in 1991. China, the USA and Northern Europe remain at the fore. The USA has won the World Cup twice, plus Olympic gold and silver medals.

### WORLD CUP HOSTS

*Europe has hosted the World Cup more times than any other continent.*

| | |
|---|---|
| 1 1930 Uruguay | 10 1974 W. Germany |
| 2 1934 Italy | 11 1978 Argentina |
| 3 1938 France | 12 1982 Spain |
| 4 1950 Brazil | 13 1986 Mexico |
| 5 1954 Switzerland | 14 1990 Italy |
| 6 1958 Sweden | 15 1994 USA |
| 7 1962 Chile | 16 1998 France |
| 8 1966 England | 17 2002 S. Korea/Japan |
| 9 1970 Mexico | 18 2006 Germany |

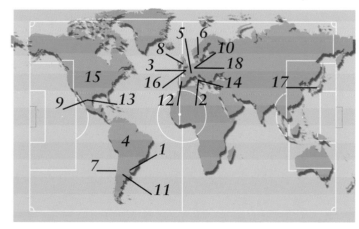

# Staying fit

**G**ood fitness training cuts down injuries and speeds up recovery when injuries do strike. You can't win matches if you can't play!

*Internationals do it, and so should you. Stretch and hold during the warm-up before the match.*

## HEALTHY EATING

Try to keep to a balanced diet by eating foods from the basic groups – dairy products, meat, fish and chicken, fruit and vegetables plus cereals, and you should absorb enough vitamins and energy. On training or match days, eat about two hours before the start, then drink liquid – plain water is best – to prevent dehydration.

## EXERCISE

By exercising, as well as practising between matches, players can increase their agility, speed and power. Over a season, a player who has an extra metre of pace could make the difference between winning and losing a championship. A player who can jump 12 cm higher could save or head a vital goal. For speed, time yourself over a 30-metre distance, then try to beat that time before the end of the week. Measure how high you can jump, arm stretched upwards, against a goal post. Aim to be higher still the next week.

## TECH TIPS – WARMING UP AND COOLING DOWN

*Warming up for about 25 minutes before a match can make all the difference when going in early for that vital tackle or racing for a ball. It also helps prevent injuries. Cooling down after prevents stiffness in the joints and muscles.*

Cool shower
2 mins moving joints
3 mins legs held in air
5 mins jogging
3 mins stretching
10 mins stretching
10 mins jumping, shooting, heading
5 mins jogging
5 mins match preparation
The match

## SKILL DRILL – THE *CARIOCA*

Aerobics in the warm-up, jogging and flex runs (like the carioca, right) help flexibility. A few minutes should be enough to raise the muscle temperature – another aid to preventing injury.

*Rapidly move sideways down a line. Cross one leg, first in front and then behind the other leg.*

*Gently swing your arms and shoulders in the opposite direction to your hips. Repeat the exercise using your other leg.*

# Glossary

CAUTION or yellow card, shown to an offending player after a foul

CORNER-KICK awarded to the attacking side when the ball goes over the goal line, but not into the goal, off a defender

DISMISSAL or red card, shown by a referee to an offending player for a serious foul, or after being shown two yellow cards in one match

FOUL tripping, kicking or barging a player

FREE KICK awarded to a player who has been fouled. A direct free kick is taken after more serious offences and can be a shot at goal. An indirect free kick after a less serious offence has to be passed before a side can shoot.

GOAL-KICK taken by the defending side after the ball has gone over the goal line, but not into the goal, off an attacking player

GOAL LINE the line at the end of the pitch running from one corner flag to the other

HANDLING only goalkeepers may handle the ball, and only in the penalty area. Penalised by a direct free kick or penalty.

OFFSIDE illegal move by attackers. Penalised by an indirect free kick.

PENALTY AREA area in front of goal in which fouls by the defence are penalised by a penalty kick

PENALTY KICK awarded to the attacking side after a foul or hand ball in the penalty area by the defence. Taken from the penalty spot, only the kicker and the goalkeeper are allowed in the area.

THE 'D' semicircle on the edge of the penalty area, inside which players must not stand during a penalty kick

THROW-IN used to restart the game after the ball has left the sides of the pitch

# Further information

The Football Association
25 Soho Square,
London,
W1D 4FA
www.thefa.com

Women's Football Alliance
25 Soho Square,
London,
W1D 4FA

English Schools FA
1/2 Eastgate Street,
Stafford,
ST16 2NN

Wales Football Association
3 Westgate Street,
Cardiff,
CF1 1DD

FIFA
PO Box 85 8030,
Zurich,
Switzerland

Scotland Football Association
Hampden Park,
Glasgow,
G42 9AY

Soccer Australia
PO Box 6038,
Silverwater,
NSW 1811

Referees' Association
1 Westhill Road,
Coundon,
CV6 2AD

UEFA
Route de Geneve 46,
Carte Postale CH 1260,
Nyon,
Switzerland

Irish Football Association
20 Windsor Avenue,
Belfast,
BT9 6EG

# Index